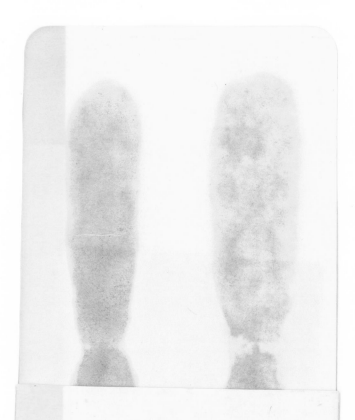

Books by W. S. Merwin

Opening the Hand

Opening the Hand

POEMS BY W. S. Merwin

New York ATHENEUM *1983*

SOME OF THESE POEMS HAVE APPEARED IN THE FOLLOWING PERIODICALS:

AMERICAN POETRY REVIEW: APPARITIONS; HIGH WATER; SHERIDAN;
    A BIRTHDAY
THE ARK: SUN AND RAIN
THE ATLANTIC: THE BRIEFCASE; GOING; DIRECTION
THE FALCON: VISITATION; THE COW
FIELD: GOING FROM THE GREEN WINDOW
GRAND STREET: EMIGRÉ
THE IOWA REVIEW: THE HOUSES; BIRDY; THE BURNT CHILD; THE SHORE; ALI;
    THE BLACK JEWEL
THE NATION: STRAWBERRIES; SON; TALKING; THE CART; PHOTOGRAPH; UNKNOWN
    FOREBEAR; THE RED HOUSE; TIDAL LAGOON; LINE OF TREES; QUESTIONS TO
    TOURISTS; HAPPENS EVERY DAY; PALM; BERRYMAN
THE NEW AMERICAN REVIEW: THE WAVING OF A HAND
THE NEW STATESMAN: YESTERDAY; A FAMILY; LATE WONDERS
THE NEW YORKER: THE OARS; SUNSET WATER; A PAUSE BY THE WATER; AFTER
    A STORM; SHAVING WITHOUT A MIRROR; GREEN WATER TOWER; COMING BACK
    IN THE SPRING; THE FIELDS; THE NIGHT SURF; THE QUOIT; JAMES; HEARING
THE ONTARIO REVIEW: THE WATERS
THE YALE REVIEW: THE MIDDLE OF SUMMER; ONE NIGHT

811
Merwin

Copyright © 1983 by W. S. Merwin
All rights reserved
Published simultaneously in Canada by McClelland and Stewart Ltd
ISBN 0–689–11383–8 (cloth); 0–689–11381–1 (paper)
LCCN 82–73495
Composed and printed by Heritage Printers, Inc., Charlotte, North Carolina
Bound by The Delmar Company, Charlotte, North Carolina
Designed by Harry Ford
First Edition

for Leon *and* Marjorie Edel

Contents

Contents

III

I

THE WATERS

I was the whole summer remembering
more than I knew
as though anything could stand still
in the waters

there were lives that turned and appeared to wait
and I went toward them looking
sounds carry in water but not
what I called so far

sun and moon shone into
the moving water
and after many days
joys and griefs I had not thought were mine

woke in this body's altering dream
knowing where they were
faces that would never die returned
toward our light through mortal waters

THE OARS

My father was born   in a house by a river
nobody knows   the color of the water
already seeds had set   in the summer weeds
the house needed paint   but nobody will see

after the century turned   he sat in a rowboat
with its end on the bank   below the house
holding onto the oars   while the trains roared past
until it was time for him   to get up and go

SUNSET WATER

How white my father looked   in the water
all his life he swam   doggie paddle
holding hurried breaths   steering an embarrassed smile

long after he has gone I rock   in smooth waves near the edge of the sea
at the foot of a hill   I never saw before
or so I imagine   as the sun is setting
sharp evening birds   and voices of children
echo each other   across the water

one by one the red waves   out of themselves reach through me

THE WAVING OF A HAND

First rose a low shore   pastures green to the water
that my father must have seen   but did he know it at the time
and maybe it seemed to him then   that he was arriving
    a few white facades   far off on the land's edge
lighthouse not yet flashing   small coast guard station
all faintly gleaming   under low sky
by the wide river mouth   late in the day
cold wind sweeping   green estuary
but everything still   calm and as it should be
    water sound sliding   close by under wood
everyone lying down   in the thin vessel
except the one sailor   leaning against the mast
face never seen   turned away forward
catching last sunlight   eyes toward the sea
waves out there suddenly blue   and sky darkening
    yet I was standing   in an old wooden house
where surely my father had stood   but had he known it then
I was among friends   he had never met
    out in back through the window   the same quiet yard
and small wooden study   beyond it under trees
it was growing dark in the room   but no one turned a light on
and the next time   I looked through that window
there was nothing to see in the yard   but a cloud
a white cloud   full of moonlight
and I tapped someone's shoulder   and we both stared
    then we talked of other things   I did not stay
soon it was really night   I ate with friends it rained
three times I climbed   a long staircase
the first time and the second   someone was at the top
    hundreds of miles   to the west
my father died   just before one in the morning

STRAWBERRIES

When my father died I saw   a narrow valley

it looked as though it began   across the river
from the landing where he was born   but there was no river

I was hoeing the sand   of a small vegetable plot
for my mother   in deepening twilight
and looked up in time   to see a farm wagon
dry and gray   horse already hidden
and no driver   going into the valley
carrying a casket

and another wagon
coming out of the valley   behind a gray horse
with a boy driving   and a high load
of two kinds of berries   one of them strawberries

that night when I slept   I dreamed of things
wrong in the house   all of them signs
the water of the shower   running brackish
and an insect of a kind   I had seen him kill
climbing around   the walls of his bathroom
up in the morning   I stopped on the stairs
my mother was awake   already and asked me
if I wanted a shower   before breakfast
and for breakfast she said   we have strawberries

A PAUSE BY THE WATER

After the days of walking   alone in mountains
between cities and after the nights   again under dripping trees
coming down I kept seeing   in my mind the ocean
though I knew it would not be   like anything I imagined

after hearing of the old man's   dying and after the burial
between rainy morning and rainy evening   the start of a cold summer
coming down the misted path alone   I kept finding
in my thought the ocean   though I told myself
step by step that it could never   be at all like that

warm simple and there   full of real day
blue and familiar   as far as the sky
breathing softly   beyond the pines and
the white unprinted   sand and I would
surely not be sailing   in that small boat
like the one I wanted   by a lake long ago

and it is true there is   this wind off the ocean
so that I shiver with   my collar up
standing on the splashed cement   of the sea wall
and through the foggy field glasses   from before the war
I can make out several   channel markers leaning
and a brace of freighters   a tug with brown barges
the faint domes of gas tanks   on the distant shore

if I did not know where I was   I could be anywhere
with that one sail   crossing the lenses
heeled over so that I   can watch the gleam of the hull
white but for one black patch   recurring between waves
as it passes in the cold of my hands   while behind me
I feel the dusk   surfacing on the swimming pool
and from the far end the eyes   of the muffled couple
in deck chairs under the petals   of frosted glass

who have been coming here   every year for years
soon we will eat our fish   in the lighted room
and later they will show me   pictures of children

SON

As the shadow closed   on the face once my father's
three times leaning forward   far off she called
Good night in a whisper   from before I was born
later through the burial   a wren went on singing

then it was that I left   for the coast to live
a single long mountain   close to the shore
from it the sun rose   and everyone there asked me
who I was   I asked them who they were

at that time I found the cave   under the mountain
drawings still on the walls   carved fragments in the dirt
all my days I spent there   groping in the floor
but some who came from nearby   were wrecking the place for a game
garbage through holes overhead   broken cars dead animals
in the evenings they rolled huge rocks   down to smash the roof
nothing that I could do   kept them from it for long

the old story   the old story

and in the mornings the cave   full of new daylight

SUN AND RAIN

Opening the book   at a bright window
above a wide pasture   after five years
I find I am still standing   on a stone bridge
looking down with my mother   at dusk into a river
hearing the current as hers   in her lifetime

now it comes to me   that that was the day
she told me of seeing my father   alive for the last time
and he waved her back from the door   as she was leaving
took her hand   for a while and said
nothing

        at some signal
in a band of sunlight all the black cows   flow down the pasture together
to turn uphill and stand   as the dark rain touches them

THE HOUSES

Up on the mountain where nobody is looking
a man forty years old in a gray felt hat
is trying to light a fire in the springtime

up on the mountain where nobody
except God and the man's son are looking
the father in a white shirt is trying
to get damp sticks to burn in the spring noon

he crumples newspaper from the luggage compartment
of the polished black Plymouth parked under the young leaves
a few feet away in the overgrown wagon track
that he remembers from another year
he is thinking of somewhere else as the match flame blows .

he has somewhere else in mind that nobody knows
as the flame climbs into the lines of print and they curl
and set out unseen into the sunlight
he needs more and more paper and more matches
and the wrapping from hot dogs and from buns
gray smoke gets away among the slender trees

it does not occur to the son to wonder
what prompted his father to come up here
suddenly this one morning and bring his son
though the father looks like a stranger on the mountain
breaking sticks and wiping his hand on the paper
as he crumples it and blowing into the flames
but when his father takes him anywhere they are both strangers

and the father has long forgotten that the son
is standing there and he is surprised
when the smoke blows in his face and he turns
and sees parallel with the brim the boy looking at him
having been told that he could not help and to wait there
and since it is a day without precedents the son
hears himself asking the father whether he may
please see what is down the wagon track and he surprises
himself hearing the father say yes but don't go far

and be very careful and come right back
so the son turns to his right and steps over
the gray stones and leaves his father making
a smoky fire on the flat sloping rock
and after a few steps the branches close overhead
he walks in the green day in the smell of thawed earth
and a while further on he comes to a turn to the right
and the open light of cleared ground falling away
still covered with the dry grass of last year
by a dark empty barn he can see light through

and before the barn on the left a white house
newly painted with wide gray steps leading
up to the gray floor of the porch where the windows
are newly washed and without curtains so that he
can look into the empty rooms and see the doors
standing open and he can look out
through windows on the other side into the sky
while the grass new and old stands deep all around the house
that is bare in readiness for somebody
the wind is louder than in the wood
the grass hissing and the clean panes rattling

he looks at rusted handles beside bushes
and with that thinks of his father and turns back
into the shadowy wagon track and walks
slowly tree by tree stone by stone under
the green tiers of leaves until he comes
to the smell of smoke and then the long pile of stones
before the clearing where his father is bending
over the fire and turns at the son's voice and calls him
a good boy for coming back and asks whether
he's hungry and holds out a paper plate
they stand in the smoke holding plates while the father
asks the blessing and afterwards the son tells him

of the white house the new paint the clean windows
into empty rooms and sky and nobody in sight
but his father says there is no such house along there
and he warns the son not to tell stories

but to eat and after a moment the son
surprises them both by insisting that he has
seen it all just as he said and again the father
scolds him this time more severely returning
from somewhere else to take up his sternness
until the son starts to cry and asks him
to come and see for himself after they have eaten

so when the plates have been burned and the fire
put out carefully and the car packed they walk
without a word down the wagon track where the light
seems to have dimmed as though rain might be on its way
and the trees are more remote than the boy
had thought but before long they reach the opening
where the track turns to the right and there is
the glare of the dry grass but no house no barn
and the son repeats I saw them but the father says
I don't want to hear any more about it

in a later year the father takes the boy
taller now and used to walking by himself
to an old farm in the middle of the state
where he busies himself in the small house he has bought
while the son having been told that he cannot help
walks down the lane past the vacant corn crib and barn
past the red shale banks where the lane descends
beside unkempt pastures with their springs and snakes
into the woods and onto a wooden bridge

still on his father's land he watches the dark water
flow out from under low branches and the small fish
flickering in glass over the black bed and as he
turns and climbs the lane on the far side he sees
to his right below him on the edge of the stream
a low house painted yellow with a wide porch
a gun leaning beside the front door and a dog's chain
fastened to the right of the steps but no dog visible

there appears to be no one in the house and the boy goes
on up the lane through the woods and across pastures

and coming back sees that nothing has changed
the gun still by the door the chain in the same place
he watches to see whether anything moves
he listens he stares through the trees wondering
where the dog is and when someone will come home

then he crosses the stream and returns to his father
indoors and in the evening he remembers
to ask who is living in the yellow house
in the woods on the far side of the stream
which he had understood was his father's land
but his father tells him there is no house there

by then they have left the farm and are driving home
and the son tells the father of the gun by the door
the dog's chain by the front steps and the father
says yes that is his land beyond the stream
but there is no building and nobody living there

the boy stops telling what he has seen
and it is a long time before he comes again
to walk down the lane to the woods and cross the bridge
and see on the far side only trees by the stream

then the farm is sold and the woods are cut and the subject
never brought up again but long after the father
is dead the son sees the two houses

APPARITIONS

Now it happens in these years   at unguarded intervals
with a frequency   never to be numbered
a motif surfacing in some scarcely known   music of my own
each time the beginning and   then broken off

that I will be looking down   not from a window
and once more catch a glimpse   of them hovering
above a whiteness like paper   and much nearer than I would have thought
lines of his knuckles   positions of his fingers
shadowy models of the backs   of my father's hands
that always appeared   to be different from my own

whether as to form texture   role or articulation
with a difference I granted them   from their origin
those stub fingers   as his family would term them
broad and unsprung   deflated somewhat and pallid
that I have seen stand forth one by one   obedient as dogs
so the scissors could cut   the flat nails straight across

they that whitened carrying   small piles of papers
and performed pretending   they knew how
posed with tools   held up neckties and waited
gripped their steering wheel   or my arm before striking
furnished him with complaints   concerning their skin and joints
evoked no music ever   had no comeliness
that I could recognize   when I yet supposed
that they were his alone   and were whole
what time they were younger   than mine are

or again the veins will appear   in their risen color
running over the hands   I knew as my mother's
that surprised me by pausing   so close to me
and I wait for the smell   of parsley and almonds
that I never imagined   otherwise than as hers

to float to me from the polished   translucent skin
and the lightness   of the tapering
well-kept and capable   poised small fingers
and from the platinum   wedding-band (with its gleam
of an outer planet)   that I have watched

finger and thumb of the other   hand slowly turn
and turn   while someone's voice was continuing

those hands that were always   on the way back to something
they that were shaken at the sink   and stripped the water
from each other like gloves   and dried swiftly on the dishtowel
flew above typewriter keys   faster than I could watch
faster than words   and without hesitation
appear again   and I am practicing the piano
that I have not touched   for as long as their age
one of them rises to wait   at the corner of the page
and I feel mistakes approach   that I have just learned not to make

but as I recognize   those hands they are gone
and that is what they are   as well as what they became
without belief I still watch them   wave to no one but me
across one last room   and from one receding car
it is six years now   since they touched anything
and whatever they can be said   to have held at all
spreads in widening rings   over the rimless surface

what I see then are these two   hands I remember
that wash my face   and tie my shoestrings
and have both sides   and a day around them
I do not know   how they came to me
they are nobody's children   who do they answer to
nobody told them to bleed   but their scars are my own
nobody but me   knows what they tell me
of flame and honey   and where you are
and the flow of water   the pencil in the air

BIRDIE

You don't think anything that I know of
but as for me when I think of you
I don't know how many of you there are
and I suppose you thought there was just the one

how many times you may have been born
as my father's other sisters would say
in your bawdy nobody is interested
in things like that in the family

somebody wrote down though that you was
born one time on April 20
1874 so that my grandmother
at that occasion was thirteen and the hardest thing
to believe in that account as I think of it
is that she was ever thirteen years old
the way we grew up to hide things from each other

so she had a little baby at that age

and that was you Birdie that was one of you
did you know
it presents a different picture of my
grandmother from the one I was brought up to

that was the you she had when she was thirteen
which goes a long way to explain
her puritanism and your gypsy earrings
and all the withered children who came after
and their scorn of your bright colors and your loud heart

and maybe even your son who was delicate
and an artist and painted heads of Jesus
on church walls where they crumbled and could not be moved
and your having a good time and dying in Arizona

except that as everybody knew
that you
was nothing but a mistake in
the writing and the real Birdie came along

when Grandma was into her twenties and she
had her firstborn a little baby girl
which explains nothing

puritanism earrings the children who came after
your son the frail artist the crumbling heads of Jesus
the having a good time and dying in Arizona
that was the you I met one morning in summer
whom nobody could explain for you was different

inviting all them so unexpected
and not heard of for so long your own mother
younger brother younger sisters new nephew
to breakfast laughing and waving your hands

with all the rings and them not listening
saying they was in a hurry to drive farther
and see the family and you going on
telling them everything there was to eat

THE BURNT CHILD

Matches among other things that were not allowed
never would be
lying high in a cool blue box
that opened in other hands and there they all were
bodies clean and smooth blue heads white crowns
white sandpaper on the sides of the box scoring
fire after fire gone before

I could hear the scratch and flare
when they were over
and catch the smell of the striking
I knew what the match would feel like
lighting
when I was very young

a fire engine came and parked
in the shadow of the big poplar tree
on Fourth Street one night
keeping its engine running
pumping oxygen to the old woman
in the basement
when she died the red lights went on burning

YESTERDAY

My friend says I was not a good son
you understand
I say yes I understand

he says I did not go
to see my parents very often you know
and I say yes I know

even when I was living in the same city he says
maybe I would go there once
a month or maybe even less
I say oh yes

he says the last time I went to see my father
I say the last time I saw my father

he says the last time I saw my father
he was asking me about my life
how I was making out and he
went into the next room
to get something to give me

oh I say
feeling again the cold
of my father's hand the last time

he says and my father turned
in the doorway and saw me
look at my wristwatch and he
said you know I would like you to stay
and talk with me

oh yes I say

but if you are busy he said
I don't want you to feel that you
have to
just because I'm here

I say nothing

he says my father
said maybe
you have important work you are doing
or maybe you should be seeing
somebody I don't want to keep you

I look out the window
my friend is older than I am
he says and I told my father it was so
and I got up and left him then
you know

though there was nowhere I had to go
and nothing I had to do

TALKING

Whatever I talk about is yesterday
by the time I see anything it is gone
the only way I can see today
is as yesterday

I talk with words I remember
about what has already happened
what I want to talk about is no longer there
it is not there

today I say only what I remember
even when I am speaking of today
nobody else remembers what I remember
not even the same names

I tell parts of a story
that once occurred
and I laugh with surprise at what disappeared
though I remember it so well

AFTER A STORM

When I come back I find
a place that was never there

once I stood where
the poplar as big as the house
shimmered with streetlight and moonlight
years before
outside the window
by my bed in the first room
and there is no tree there
and the house has no door

again amazed to be alone so young
one time in the country I climbed a hill
to see the night pasture
in the afternoon in spring
and the hollow and deep woods
beyond the bright grass

lying on the white boards
of the leaky boat
that I had dragged up from the lake bottom
after lifting the stones out
and then dried in the sun
and caulked and tarred
and found a mast for in spring
I went on looking up
at the sky above the mast
no breath of wind no cloud
lake water lapping the painted chamber

not even the last to go
are water sounds
wild brooks in the woods
clear streams full of beings
unknown flowers
the doors of water
are not even the last to close
the bells of water not yet the last bells

there are the doors of no water
the bells of no water
the bells of air
if I could take one voice
with me it would be
the sound I hear every day

THE CART

One morning in summer
music flew up out of New
York Avenue
under the bay window

down there a small man called
a foreigner
one hand on the nose of a horse
no taller than he was

and a cart behind them with wooden
wheels tight to the curb
by the street car tracks
were facing upstream waiting

on the cart a rocking
tower as big as a kitchen
with a round pointed roof
hung over the edges

yellow trellises all around
red painted chairs inside
one behind another
circling with the music

the horse was small for the cart
the cart was small for the tower
the tower was small for the chairs
the chairs were small for us

the circle was large for the tower
the tower was large for the cart
the tower was large for the street
the street was large for us

but we sat in the music
and went round over nothing
as long as we could
and the street car came by

The Cart

as we turned and it passed us
with faces at all the windows
looking out
knowing us

PHOTOGRAPH

After he died
they found the picture
that he had kept looking for
and had thought was lost
all those years

they did not know
how it had hung in the mind
of someone who could not find it
they did not even
know whose face
that was supposed to be

UNKNOWN FORBEAR

Somebody who knew him
ninety years ago
called him by a name
he answered to
come out now they said to him
onto the porch and stand
right there

it was summer and the nine windows
that they could see
were open all the way
so was the front door
and the curtains faded as aprons hung
limp past the sills while he stood
there alone in his dark suit
and white beard in the sunshine

he appeared to know where he was
whose porch that was and whose
house behind him
younger than he was
and who had opened the windows

and who had left the ladder
propped in the branches up the lane
and the names of his children and their children
and the name of the place
with the pine tree out front
and the mullein a foot high growing
on the green bank
beyond the stones of the walk

as he stood still looking out
through the opening in the painted
picket fence
one tall picket one short picket
all the way along

and no gate in the opening

A FAMILY

Would you believe me
if I told you the name of the farmers
at the end of the lake
where it grew shallow over the mossy rocks

and if you came in the morning the grass was blue
the fur of the rocks was wet the small frogs jumped
and the lake was silent behind you
except for echoes

you tied your boat carefully to a tree
before setting out across the cool pasture
watching for the bull
all the way to the barn

or if you came in the afternoon
the pasture glared and hummed the dark leaves smelled
from beside the water and the barn was drunk
by the time you got to it

to climb on the beams
to dive into the distant hay
will you believe
the names of the farmer's children

II

SHAVING WITHOUT A MIRROR

As though there could be more   than one center
many skies cleared in the night   and there it is
the mountain this face of it   still brindled with cloud shadows
if I raised my hand   I could touch it like air
high shallow valleys   cradling the clear wind
all like a thing remembered   where haystacks waited for winter

but now it is so blue   would there be eyes in it
looking out from dark nerves   as the morning passes in our time
while the sound of a plane rises   behind me beyond trees
so that I breathe and reach up to the air   and feel water
it is myself   the listener to the music
to the clouds in the gray passes   and the clear leaves

where are the forest voices   now that the forests have gone
and those from above the treeline   oh where that fed on fog
of a simpler compound   that satisfied them
when did I ever knowingly   set hands on a cloud
who have walked in one often   following the rim in anger
Brother the world is blind   *and surely you come from it*
where children grow steadily   without knowledge of creatures

other than domesticated   though rags of woods yet emerge
as the clouds part and sweep on   passing southward in spring
fingers crossing the slopes   shadows running leaping
all night that peak watched   the beacon over the sea
and answered nothing   now it turns to the morning
an expression of knowledge   above immigrant woods

nothing is native of fire   and everything is born of it
then I wash my face   as usual
trying to remember a date   before the war
coming to a green farm at sunrise   dew smell from pastures
after that there were various   graduations
this passion for counting   has no root of its own
I stand by a line of trees   staring at a bare summit
do I think I was born here   I was never born

VISITATION

Two natives of the bare mountains   appear in the doorway
first I saw the dogs coming   far down the gold slope

the men shuffle and say hello   rimmed with sunlight
and ask if I've seen anything   up here all morning
winds of autumn are passing   over the uplands
migrations of shadows   crossing dry grass
clouds keep running the wall   of dark peaks to the south
ragged flocks trail   through the calling sky

but these had in mind   the animals
had I seen them at all   that made the hoofprints
or a sign of the hare   the quail or the partridge
no I tell them   and they nod and look away

how do I like it   up here they ask
but they won't come in   they were just passing
don't mind the dogs they say   and they tell me
the name of where they came from   and step from the doorway

every year they say   it's harder to find them
the animals   even up here
and I say is that true   and they laugh

THE RED HOUSE

Room after room without a voice   no one to say
only another century   could afford so much space
spring sunlight through locked shutters   reveals the old patchworks
adrift on the old beds   in the dry air
and in the white fireplaces   already it is summer

but there is only one age   in all the rooms and mirrors
and it is beginning   it has come to begin
the sound of a bus arrives outside   and what looks like a closet door
in an upstairs bedroom opens   onto green woods
full of the thin leaves of May   and a shimmering meadow
and deep in grass   beyond a stream and a waterfall
the rusted windowless bus   to the amber fields

TIDAL LAGOON

From the edge of the bare reef   in the afternoon
children who can't swim   fling themselves forward calling
and disappear for a moment   in the long mirror
that contains the reflections   of the mountains

GREEN WATER TOWER

A guest at Thanksgiving   said And you've got
a green water tower   with a blue two painted on it

it is there at the edge of the woods   on the hill to the east
at night it flattens   into the black profile of trees
clouds bloom from behind it   moonlight climbs through them
to the sound of pouring   far inside

in an east wind we wake hearing it   wondering where it is
above it the sky grows pale   white sun emerges
the green tower swells   in rings of shadow
day comes   we drink and stand listening

HIGH WATER

The river is rising   with the beathless sound of a fever
the wake along each shore   trembles and is torn away
a few steps up in the rain   rows of white faces
watch from the banks   backs to the cellar doors

behind the blue eyes   are the cellars' contents
silent in bottles   each with its date
on shelves waiting   under the dripping hats

when the faces draw closer   to each other in the rain
they talk like members   of one family
telling what could be moved   if they have to move it
saying where would be safe   talking of the gardens on the hills
the rains other years   what most needs repair
what the spring   means to the summer

even of the lake in the mountains   which they own together
and agree once again   never to sell

LINE OF TREES

Along the west of the woods   is a row of tall pines
the man who planted them   came from an island
thousands of miles to the south   and now with his wife
for a long time a nurse   but lately not right in the head
who came from an island   thousands of miles from his
he lives down the road   since their small house in the woods
burned beyond repair   but he still comes by
every so often   to ignore the mailbox
rusted sedan full of vines   brown fruit in the grassy ruts
and when he has gone a pheasant   barks from hiding
bird of a far continent   and whenever the boughs
part suddenly to reveal the yellow   house wall with its window
what they show is a mirror   full of western light

A HOUSE TO THE WEST

Day of harsh south wind built up the black clouds
but no rain fell and near sunset
the air turned still and full of afterlight

on the ridge to the west the tin barn in the trees
the well-digger's derrick
the plywood shack the color of clotted blood
settle onto the gray sky

the bony woman blond all her life
whose house that is
the woman named for a star
screams at her dog
calls baby talk to her goats
and far from the traffic where she was born
she turns into a shadow among fence posts

when the lovers and children had all got clear of her voice
she said of the red shack It is mine
and she got a driver to move it
one fine morning out onto the hill beyond everything
and then couldn't believe it
and never lights a lamp

THE COW

The two boys down the road   with a vegetable farm
they started from scratch   for their religion
say they didn't known anything   when they began
they had to pick it up   as they went along
all about growing things   and they made a lot of mistakes
said they never knew   much about animals
but their benefactor   bought these cows for the pasture
only the one is a bull   without any balls
and the one is a cow   but she's too young still
and the only one   that's been in milk
was Mama Cow   and they learned to milk her
the whole three were got cheap   going to slaughter
and she wasn't considered   to be much of a milker
but they got most days   a gallon and a half
some days two   all through the summer
good milk too   better than what you buy
then the rains started   but it made no difference
there was a shed roof   all three could get under
but they all seemed to like   to hang out in the rain
just all the time   standing in the rain
then her milk all at once   began to go down
in a couple of days   it was right to nothing
then she got hold   of some dried apples they had
until she wouldn't   eat any more
and made it down   to the bottom of the pasture
to the mud hole   and lay down in the mud
and then couldn't get up   that's where they found her
she couldn't hardly   lift her head up
she was breathing heavy   they thought it was the apples
she looked so swollen   lying on her side
and she didn't get up   that whole day
so they sent for the vet   along late in the afternoon
he drove up   as the sun was going down
they opened the gate in the wires   at milking time
he brought the truck   into the pasture
he stepped down   at the edge of the mud
Picked a bad place to lie   lady he told her
listened to her all over   through a rubber tube
across the mud   and took her temperature
It wasn't the apples   he stood up and told them

The Cow

she had pneumonia   weak with the fever
they'd have to move her   out of that mud there
they fastened to the horns first   and the truck tugged until a horn broke
he said he'd known a dragged horse   to leave all four hooves in the mud
they tried with the same rope   to the front legs and back legs
they dragged her along   to where it was anyways dry
he gave her some shots   showing them how
she tried to get up   but she fell right back
head down on the ground   on the broken horn
the moon at first quarter   gathering light
above the rain clouds   at the top of the hill
he said it was better   not to cover her
unless they were going   to sit up beside her
to keep the cover   from slipping off in the night
then he left   turning his lights on
in a few minutes   it started to rain
and they went out too   in a little while
to see a friend   and were not away long
but when they came back   she was gone lying there
she looked as though   she must be alive
with her eye open   in the moonlight
but when they touched her   it hit them for sure
Heavy they said   she was so big
they said they never   knew she was so big
and they saw dead things   every day
they couldn't believe it   at first they said
all the next morning   trying to burn her
with old tires   but they gave that up
and brought dirt   and piled it on her
That's what it's about   one of them said
Life and death isn't it   what it's about
and the other said   that after what they'd fed her
the blessings on the food   and the scriptures she'd heard
she was almost sure to be   reborn already
in human form   in a family of their faith

42

QUESTIONS TO TOURISTS STOPPED
BY A PINEAPPLE FIELD

Did you like your piece of pineapple   would you like a napkin
who gave you the pineapple   what do you know about them
do you eat much pineapple   where you come from
how did this piece compare   with pineapple you have eaten before
what do you remember about the last time   you ate a piece of pineapple
did you know where it came from   how much did it cost
do you remember the first time   you tasted pineapple
do you like it better fresh   or from the can
what do you remember   of the picture on the can
what did you feel   as you looked at the picture
which do you like better   the picture or the pineapple field
did you ever imagine   pineapples growing somewhere

how do you like   these pineapple fields
have you ever seen   pineapple fields before
do you know whether pineapple   is native to the islands
do you know whether the natives   ate pineapple
do you know whether the natives   grew pineapple
do you know how the land was acquired   to be turned into pineapple fields
do you know what is done to the land   to turn it into pineapple fields
do you know how many months   and how deeply they plow it
do you know what those machines do   are you impressed
do you know what is in those containers   are you interested

what do you think was here   before the pineapple fields
would you suppose that the fields   represent an improvement
do you think they smell better   than they did before
what is your opinion   of those square miles of black plastic
where do you think the plastic   goes when the crop is over
what do you think becomes of the land   when the crop is over
do you think the growers know best   do you think this is for your own good

what and where was the last   bird you noticed
do you remember   what sort of bird it was
do you know whether   there were birds here before
are there any birds   where you come from
do you think it matters   what do you think matters more
have you seen any   natives since you arrived

43

what were they doing   what were they wearing
what language were they speaking   were they in nightclubs
are there any natives   where you come from

have you taken pictures   of the pineapple fields
would you like for me   to hold the camera
so that you can all   be in the picture
would you mind   if I took your picture
standing in front   of those pineapple fields
do you expect   to come back

what made you decide   to come here
was this what   you came for
when did you first   hear of the islands
where were you then   how old were you
did you first see the islands   in black and white
what words were used   to describe the islands
what do the words mean   now that you are here
what do you do   for a living
what would you say is   the color of pineapple leaves
when you look at things in rows   how do you feel
would you like to dream   of pineapple fields

is this your first visit   how do you like the islands
what would you say   in your own words
you like best   about the islands
what do you want   when you take a trip
when did you get here   how long will you be staying
did you buy any clothes   especially for the islands
how much did you spend on them   before you came
was it easy to find clothes   for the islands
how much have you spent on clothes   since you got here
did you make your own plans   or are you part of a group
would you rather be on your own   or with a group
how many are in your group   how much was your ticket
are the side-tours part of the ticket   or are they extra
are hotel and meals and car   part of the ticket or extra
have you already paid   or will you pay later
did you pay by check   or by credit card
is this car rented   by the day or week

how does it compare   with the one you drive at home
how many miles   does it do to a gallon
how far do you   want to go on this island

where have you been   in the last three hours
what have you seen   in the last three miles
do you feel hurried   on your vacation
are you getting   your money's worth
how old are you   are you homesick are you well
what do you eat here   is it what you want
what gifts are you planning   to take back
how much do you expect   to spend on them
what have you bought   to take home with you
have you decided   where to put each thing
what will you say   about where they came from
what will you say   about the pineapple fields

do you like dancing here   what do you do when it rains
was this trip   purely for pleasure
do you drink more   or less than at home
how do you like   the place where you live now
were you born there   how long have you lived there
what does the name mean   is it a growth community
why are you living there   how long do you expect to stay
how old is your house   would you like to sell it

in your opinion   coming from your background
what do the islands offer   someone of your age
are there any changes   you would like to promote
would you like to invest here   would you like to live here
if so would it be year round   or just for part of the year
do you think there is a future   in pineapple

THE BRIEFCASE

He came from the far north   I can name the country
gray hair cropped   to the shape of his skull
good gray suit   perfectly pressed
on his sharp shoulders   and from a long sleeve
thin hand in leather   hooked to a briefcase
and never looked at me   as he walked past
how then do I know   the voice and accent
I've seen him before   from time to time
now I try to remember   what happened next each time
and I've heard what his work is   thinker and planner
administrator   of a model camp
what kind of camp   nobody could say
and he's on his way from there   right now as I watch him
disappear once more   behind a building
while leaves rustle   over my head
in the evening   and lights come on

LATE WONDERS

In Los Angeles the cars are flowing
through the white air
and the news of bombings

at Universal Studios
you can ride through an avalanche
if you have never
ridden through an avalanche

with your ticket
you can ride on a trolley
before which the Red
Sea parts
just the way it did
for Moses

you can see Los Angeles
destroyed hourly
you can watch the avenue named for somewhere else
the one on which you know you are
crumple and vanish incandescent
with a terrible cry
all around you
rising from the houses and families
of everyone you have seen all day
driving shopping talking eating

it's only a movie
it's only a beam of light

GOING

Feet waiting in pairs   ways of sitting in subways
through all ages   ways of waiting
thinking of something else   that is elsewhere
iron carriages all day   flying through night
positions of daily papers   held up to be read
same papers flying in parks   rising above trees
are reflected once in glass   unknown glass
and in spilled water before   feet hurrying homeward

STANDING NOWHERE

When I come home in the city   and see the young roaches
running on the bare cliffs   they pause to see what I am
delaying their going   without company over unmapped spaces
feet finding their way   from black eggs small as dust
it is true that they do not know   anything about me
nor where we are from   we can have
little knowledge   we look at each other and wait
whatever we may do   afterwards

COMING BACK IN THE SPRING

When I turn my head in the afternoon
there are the receding files
of tall buildings blue in the distance
with amber light along them ending
in amber light
and their sides shining above the river of cars
and I am home

here are the faces the faces
the cool leaves still lucent before summer
the voices
I am home before the lights come on
home when the thunder begins after dark
and the rain in the streets at night
while the iron train again
rumbles under the sidewalk
long cans full of light and
unseen faces disappearing
in my mind

many travelling behind the same headline
saying second
IRA hunger striker dies
in British hands in Ireland
and some ingesting the latest
smiling sentencing
from the face in the White House
whose syllables wither species and places
into deaths going before us
as the print turns to the day's killings
around the planet

the words flowing under the place on the Avenue
where the truck ran over
two small boys at the intersection
Friday killing
both by the corner where the garden has been bulldozed
that flowered there for years
after the Loew's movie house was torn down
where the old pictures played

the trains rattle under the hooves
of the mounted police riding
down the Avenue at eleven in blue helmets
and past the iron skeleton
girders and stairs and sky
of the new tower risen
out of the gutted core
of St. Vincent's Hospital
most beautiful
of cities and most empty
pure Avenue behind the words of friends
and the known music

the stars are flaking in the apartment ceiling
and the lights of lives
are reflected crossing the floating night
the rain beats on the panes
above the Avenue
where I have watched it run
for twelve years in the spring
ambulances shreik among the trucks

this is an emergency the walkers
in the street in ones and twos
walk faster
those in groups walk more slowly
the white tower beyond Union Square
is lit up blue and white
during the first few
hours of darkness

we all sleep high off the ground

HAPPENS EVERY DAY

Right in midtown   walking in broad daylight
people around   and everything
all at once   this guy steps out
in front of him   and has a gun
grabs his briefcase   takes off with it
everybody around   is in a hurry
the first guy wakes up   to shout and the other one
starts running and the first guy   right after him
and the one with the briefcase   drops the gun
and the first guy   stops to pick it up
but people are passing   in between
he keeps on shouting   and barging through them
and the guy up ahead   drops the briefcase
so he starts after that   and sees somebody
gather up the gun   and get out of there
and when he stops where   he saw the briefcase
somebody else   has picked that up and gone
the other guy's vanished   and he stands looking
up and down the street   with the people
moving through him   from no beginning

SHERIDAN

The battle ended   the moment you got there

oh it was over it was over   in smoke
melted and the smoke still   washing the last away
of the shattered ends   the roaring fray
cannons gun carriages cavalry   fringes of infantry
seeping out of woods   blood bones breakage breaking
gone as though you   had just opened your eyes
and there was nobody   who saw what you had come to see
no face that realized   that you had arrived
no one in sight who knew   about you
how solid you were   General and how still
what were you doing   at last standing there
slightly smaller than life-size   in memory of yourself

this was certainly the place   there is no
place like this   this is the only place
it could have been   this unquestionably
is where the message came from   meant for you only
the touched intelligence rushing   to find you
tracing you gasping   drowning for lack of you
racing with shadows   of falling bodies
hunting you while the hours   ran and the first day
swung its long gates for cows   coming home to barnyards
fields were flooded with evening   seasons were resolved
forests came shouldering back   and the rounds
from the beginning   unrolled out of themselves
you were born and began to learn   what you learned
and it was going to find you   in your own time

with its torn phrases   to inform you
sir of your absence   to say it had happened
even then was happening   you were away
and they had broken upon   you they were long past
your picket lines they were at large   in your positions
outflanking outweighing   overrunning you
burning beyond your campfires   in your constellations
while the cows gave milk   and the country slept
and you continued there   in the crystal distance
you considered yours   until the moment

when the words turned it   to colored paper
then to painted glass   then to plain lantern glass
through which you could see   as you set your left
foot in the stirrup   the enemy
you had first imagined   flashing on the farmland

and what had become of   you all that while
who were you in the war   in the only night
then hands let go the black horse   the black road opened
all its miles   the stars on your coat went out
you were hurtling into the dark   and only the horse could see
I know because afterward   it was read to me
already in bed   my mother in the chair beside me
cellos in the avenue   of a lighted city
night after night again   I listened to your ride
as somebody never there   had celebrated it
and you did not see the road   on which you were going
growing out of itself   like a fingernail
you never saw the air   you were flying through
you never heard the hoofbeats   under you

all the way hearkening   to what was not there
one continuous mumbled   thunder collapsing
on endless stairs from   so far coming in the dark yet so
sure how could it have failed   to carry to you
calling finally by name   and how could you
in the meantime have heard nothing   but it was still not
that night's battle beyond its hills   that you were hearing
and attending to   bright before you
as a furnace mouth that kept falling   back forward away
filling with hands and known faces   that flared up and crumbled
in flowing coals   to rise then and form once more
and come on again living   so that you saw them
even when the crash of cannons   was close in the dawn
and day was breaking   all around you

a line of fence ran toward you   looking familiar
a shuttered house in the mist   you thought in passing
you remembered from some other time   so you seemed to know
where you were   my God the fighting

was almost to there already   you could hear
rifles echoing just down the road   and what sounded
like shouting and you could   smell it in the morning
where your own were watching for you   coming to meet you
horses neighing   and at once the night
had not happened behind you   the whole ride
was nothing out of which they   were hurrying you
on the white horse   telling you everything
that you had not seen could not see   never would see
taking you to the place   where you dismounted
and turned to look   at what you had come for

there was the smoke   and someone with your head
raised an arm toward it   someone with your mouth
gave an order   and stepped into the century
and is seen no more   but is said
to have won that battle   survived that war
died and been buried   and only you are there
still seeing it disappear   in front of you
everyone knows the place   by your name now
the iron fence   dry drinking fountain
old faces from brick buildings   out for some sun
sidewalk drunks   corner acquaintances
leaves luminous above you   in the city night
subway station   hands at green news stand
traffic waiting   for the lights to change

THE FIELDS

Saturday on Seventh Street
full-waisted gray-haired women in Sunday sweaters
moving through the tan shades of their booths
bend over cakes they baked at home
they gaze down onto the sleep of stuffed cabbages
they stir with huge spoons sauerkraut and potato dumplings
cooked as those dishes were cooked on deep
misty plains among the sounds of horses
beside fields of black earth on the other side of the globe
that only the oldest think they remember
looking down from their windows into the world
where everybody is now

none of the young has yet wept at the smell
of cabbages
those leaves all face
none of the young after long journeys
weeks in vessels
and staring at strange coasts through fog in first light
has been recognized by the steam of sauerkraut
that is older than anyone living
so on the street they play the music
of what they do not remember
they sing of places they have not known
they dance in new costumes under the windows
in the smell of cabbages from fields
nobody has seen

III

PALM

The palm is in no hurry
to be different
and it grows slowly
it knows how to be a palm
when it was a seed it knew
how to be a palm seed
when it was a flower
it knew how to be
the flower of a palm
when it was a palm it grew
slowly
and without eyes
in a salt wind

THE SHORE

How can anyone know that a whale
two hundred years ago could hear another
whale at the opposite end of the earth
or tell how long the eyes
of a whale have faced both halves of the world
and have found light far down in old company

with the sounds of hollow iron charging
clanging through the oceans and with the circuitries
and the harpoons of humans
and the poisoning of the seas
a whale can hear no farther through the present
than a jet can fly in a few minutes

in the days of their hearing the great Blues gathered like clouds
the sunlight under the sea's surfaces sank
into their backs as into the water around them
through which they flew invisible from above
except as flashes of movement
and they could hear each other's voices wherever they went

once it is on its own a Blue can wander
the whole world beholding both sides of the water
raising in each ocean the songs of the Blues
that it learned from distances it can no longer hear
it can fly all its life without ever meeting another Blue
this is what we are doing this is the way we sing oh Blue Blue

THE NIGHT SURF

Of tomorrow I have nothing to say
what I say is not tomorrow

tomorrow no animals
no trees growing at their will
no one in the White House
the words gone out

the end of our grasp and rage
and of our knowledge
what is between us and tomorrow

in the deep shade blue irises are open
we are barefoot in the airy house
after dark the surf roars on the cliffs

THE QUOIT

The iron ring
rose into the twilight
of late summer
the day still blue
no stars

it rose like a shadow
lit from underneath
the leaves were hanging motionless
on the big poplar
already full of night
and the voices had dropped at dusk

on a table by a new window
in an old house with no lights on
a black metal panther
glared through the black hollyhocks
toward the group of men standing under floodlamps
beside four boxes of wet clay

they had a right to their game
on coal company property
that could not be built on
in case the company
needed to sink a shaft to the mine
in a hurry

those years often the nights smelled of autumn
and people said to each other in the mornings
did you hear it last night
late
was it blasting again someone would ask
no someone else would answer
it was pickaxes

THE MIDDLE OF SUMMER

By now you have envisaged
in lives as many as those
of a tree in spring
the summer nights
in the cabin by the lake
with the sun never setting

the fire on the beach
through the endless hours of sunset
and have held the sound of the north dome
of the planet turning
gazing constantly at the sun

the lull of the lakes at that
time the hum of the surfaces
the breath of woods
bird voices clattering
through the sleepless light
of the sun at midnight
and your long shadow walking
on the still water

that is what you go on seeing
at that latitude
as the water turns silent and then
begins to tremble

JAMES

News comes that a friend far away
is dying now

I look up and see small flowers appearing
in spring grass outside the window
and can't remember their name

BERRYMAN

I will tell you what he told me
in the years just after the war
as we then called
the second world war

don't lose your arrogance yet he said
you can do that when you're older
lose it too soon and you may
merely replace it with vanity

just one time he suggested
changing the usual order
of the same words in a line of verse
why point out a thing twice

he suggested I pray to the Muse
get down on my knees and pray
right there in the corner and he
said he meant it literally

it was in the days before the beard
and the drink but he was deep
in tides of his own through which he sailed
chin sideways and head tilted like a tacking sloop

he was far older than the dates allowed for
much older than I was he was in his thirties
he snapped down his nose with an accent
I think he had affected in England

as for publishing he advised me
to paper my wall with rejection slips
his lips and the bones of his long fingers trembled
with the vehemence of his view about poetry

he said the great presence
that permitted everything and transmuted it
in poetry was passion
passion was genius and he praised movement and invention

I had hardly begun to read
I asked how can you ever be sure
that what you write is really
any good at all and he said you can't

you can't you can never be sure
you die without knowing
whether anything you wrote was any good
if you have to be sure don't write

A BIRTHDAY

Something continues and   I don't know what to call it
though the language is full of suggestions
in the way of language
                              but they are all anonymous
and it's almost your birthday   music next to my bones

these nights we hear the horses   running in the rain
it stops and the moon comes out   and we are still here
the leaks in the roof go on dripping   after the rain has passed
smell of ginger flowers   slips through the dark house
down near the sea   the slow heart of the beacon flashes

the long way to you is still tied to me   but it brought me to you
I keep wanting to give you   what is already yours
it is the morning   of the mornings together
breath of summer   oh my found one
the sleep in the same current   and each waking to you

when I open my eyes   you are what I wanted to see

THE SEA CLIFFS AT KAILUA
IN DECEMBER

Down on the tongue of black rock
where the long waves break
a young woman stands with a baby named Mist
we sit in the sun by the crag
spray blowing high into the fans of the hala trees
friends talk of how the age that is ours
came to the islands
where there were kings
in a few hours none of us will be here
the voices of the children fly up from rock pools
clouds move in from the sea
voices grow distant
a bright fish gasps on a stone near the fire
there are ghosts in the steep valley
through the years we have been along the wild coast
headland by headland
but never here

ALI

Small dog named for a wing
never old and never young

abandoned with your brothers on a beach
when you were scarcely weaned

taken home starving
by one woman with
too many to feed as it was

handed over to another
who tied you out back in the weeds
with a clothesline and fed you if she remembered

on the morning before the eclipse of the moon
I first heard about you over the telephone

only the swellings of insect bites
by then held the skin away from your bones

thin hair matted filthy the color of mud
naked belly crusted with sores
head low frightened silent watching

I carried you home and gave you milk and food
bathed you and dried you

dressed your sores and sat with you
in the sun with your wet head on my leg

we had one brother of yours already
and had named him for the great tree of the islands
we named you for the white shadows
behind your thin shoulders

and for the reminder of the desert
in your black muzzle lean as an Afghan's

and for the lightness of your ways
not the famished insubstance of your limbs

but even in your sickness and weakness
when you were hobbled with pain and exhaustion

an aerial grace a fine buoyancy
a lifting as in the moment before flight

I keep finding why that is your name

the plump vet was not impressed with you
and guessed wrong for a long time
about what was the matter

so that you could hardly eat
and never grew like your brother

small dog wise in your days

never servile never disobedient
and never far

standing with one foot on the bottom stair
hoping it was bedtime

standing in the doorway looking up
tail swinging slowly below sharp hip bones

toward the end you were with us whatever we did

the gasping breath through the night
ended an hour and a half before daylight

the gray tongue hung from your mouth
we went on calling you holding you

feeling the sudden height

THE SCHOOL ON THE ROOF

Up there day and night for weeks   they turn to water
turn themselves into water   of day water of night
clouds travel across them   rain vanishes into them
when wind stops they grow clear   birds come and are gone in them
sun rises and sets in them   their stars come out
until they come down   come down
some all the colors   of lakes and rivers
some so you can't   see them at all

GOING FROM THE GREEN WINDOW

Saying to the square that is always open good-bye
is uprooting my own foot
I never remembered the root starting
there is nothing to say good-bye to

In a room of wind and unabiding
in mid-air like a leg walking
in a turning place where boxes have stayed packed for years
where in storms the walls bleed
over the flooded floors
where at all hours constellations
of black cows wait round about
growing on the hill of grass

I watch through dark leaves once
those shadows in the day pasture
moving slowly to drink on the way to the big tree
this morning

THE TRUTH OF DEPARTURE

With each journey it gets
worse
what kind of learning is that
when that is what we are born for

and harder and harder to find
what is hanging on
to what
all day it has been raining
and I have been writing letters
the pearl curtains
stroking the headlands
under immense dark clouds
the valley sighing with rain
everyone home and quiet

what will become of all these
things that I see
that are here and are me
and I am none of them
what will become
of the bench and the teapot
the pencils and the kerosene lamps
all the books all the writing
the green of the leaves
what becomes of the house
and the island
and the sound of your footstep

who knows it is here
who says it will stay
who says I will know it
who said it would be alright

ONE NIGHT

I ride a great horse climbing
    out of a rose cloud
        onto a black cinder mountain

long ago and a horn is blowing
    and far ahead the light
        answers

EMIGRÉ

You will find it is
much as you imagined
in some respects
which no one can predict
you will be homesick
at times for something you can describe
and at times without being able to say
what you miss
just as you used to feel when you were at home

some will complain from the start
that you club together
with your own kind
but only those who have
done what you have done
conceived of it longed for it
lain awake waiting for it
and have come out with
no money no papers nothing
at your age
know what you have done
what you are talking about
and will find you a roof and employers

others will say from the start
that you avoid
those of your country
for a while
as your country becomes
a category in the new place
and nobody remembers the same things
in the same way
and you come to the problem
of what to remember after all
and of what is your real
language
where does it come from what does it
sound like
who speaks it

if you cling to the old usage
do you not cut yourself off
from the new speech
but if you rush to the new lips
do you not fade like a sound cut off
do you not dry up like a puddle
is the new tongue to be trusted

what of the relics of your childhood
should you bear in mind pieces
of dyed cotton and gnawed wood
lint of voices untranslatable stories
summer sunlight on dried paint
whose color continues to fade in the
growing brightness of the white afternoon
ferns on the shore of the transparent lake
or should you forget them
as you float between ageless languages
and call from one to the other who you are

WHAT IS MODERN

Are you modern

is the first
tree that comes
to mind modern
does it have modern leaves

who is modern after hours
at the glass door
of the drugstore
or
within sound of the airport

or passing the
animal pound
where once a week I
gas the animals
who is modern in bed

when
was modern born
who first was pleased
to feel modern
who first claimed the word
as a possession
saying I'm
modern

as someone might say
I'm a champion
or I'm
famous or even
as some would say I'm
rich

or I love the sound
of the clarinet
yes so do I
do you like classical
or modern

did modern
begin to be modern
was there a morning
when it was there for the first time
completely modern

is today modern
the modern sun rising
over the modern roof
of the modern hospital
revealing the modern water tanks and aerials
of the modern horizon

and modern humans
one after the other
solitary and without speaking
buying the morning paper
on the way to work

DIRECTION

All I remember of the long lecture
which is all I remember of one summer
are the veins on the old   old bald head
and the loose white sleeve   and bony finger pointing
beyond the listeners
over their heads

there was the dazzling   wall and the empty sunlight
and reaching out of his age he told them
for the last time
what to do when they got to the world
giving them his every breath   to take with them like water
as they vanished

nobody was coming back that way

THE NEW SEASON

On the third night of autumn
hearing rats in the dry
brush and leaves under the big trees
below the house
I go down with one of the dogs
to frighten them away

where the end of the house
looms high off the ground
we look down the dark slope
with a flashlight
listening
what was it
old dog old good heart
old Roland not too bright
only one eye

in the black
blossoms go on falling
from the Christmasberry trees
like the dripping after rain
small unseen colorless
blossoms ticking
but the bees are not there

worms are awake under the leaves
beetles are awake eating
upside down in the dark
leaves are awake hearing
in the complete night

I stand with a flashlight
in a smell of fruit
and we wait

HEARING

Back when it took all day to come up
from the curving broad ponds on the plains
where the green-winged jaçanas ran on the lily pads

easing past tracks at the mouths of gorges
crossing villages silted in hollows
in the foothills
each with its lime-washed church by the baked square
of red earth and its
talkers eating fruit under trees

turning a corner and catching
sight at last of inky forests far above
steep as faces
with the clouds stroking them and the glimmering
airy valleys opening out of them

waterfalls still roared from the folds
of the mountain
white and thundering and spray drifted
around us swirling into the broad leaves
and the waiting boughs

once I took a tin cup and climbed
the sluiced rocks and mossy branches beside
one of the high falls
looking up step by step into
the green sky from which rain was falling
when I looked back from a ledge there were only
dripping leaves below me
and flowers

beside me the hissing
cataract plunged into the trees
holding on I moved closer
left foot on a rock in the water
right foot on a rock in deeper water
at the edge of the fall
then from under the weight of my right foot
came a voice like a small bell singing

over and over one clear treble
syllable

I could feel it move
I could feel it ring in my foot in my skin
everywhere
in my ears in my hair
I could feel it in my tongue and in the hand
holding the cup
as long as I stood there it went on
without changing

when I moved the cup
still it went on
when I filled the cup
in the falling column
still it went on
when I drank it rang in my eyes
through the thunder curtain

when I filled the cup again
when I raised my foot
still it went on
and all the way down
from wet rock to wet rock
green branch to green branch
it came with me

until I stood
looking up and we drank
the light water
and when we went on we could
still hear the sound
as far as the next turn on the way over

THE BLACK JEWEL

In the dark
there is only the sound of the cricket

south wind in the leaves
is the cricket
so is the surf on the shore
and the barking across the valley

the cricket never sleeps
the whole cricket is the pupil of one eye
it can run it can leap it can fly
in its back the moon
crosses the night

there is only one cricket
when I listen

the cricket lives in the unlit ground
in the roots
out of the wind
it has only the one sound

before I could talk
I heard the cricket
under the house
then I remembered summer

mice too and the blind lightning
are born hearing the cricket
dying they hear it
bodies of light turn listening to the cricket
the cricket is neither alive nor dead
the death of the cricket
is still the cricket
in the bare room the luck of the cricket
echoes

W. S. Merwin

W. S. Merwin was born in New York City in 1927 and grew up in Union City, New Jersey, and in Scranton, Pennsylvania. From 1949 to 1951 he worked as a tutor in France, Portugal, and Majorca. After that, for several years he made the greater part of his living by translating from French, Spanish, Latin and Portuguese. Since 1954 several fellowships have been of great assistance. In addition to poetry, he has written articles, chiefly for *The Nation*, and radio scripts for the BBC. He has lived in Spain, England, France, Mexico and Hawaii, as well as New York City. His books of poetry are *A Mask for Janus* (1952), *The Dancing Bears* (1954), *Green with Beasts* (1956), *The Drunk in the Furnace* (1960), *The Moving Target* (1963), *The Lice* (1967), *The Carrier of Ladders* (1970) for which he was awarded the Pulitzer Prize, *Writings to an Unfinished Accompaniment* (1973), *The Compass Flower* (1977) and *Opening the Hand* (1983). His translations include *The Poem of the Cid* (1959), *Spanish Ballads* (1960), *The Satires of Persius* (1961), *Lazarillo de Tormes* (1962), *The Song of Roland* (1963), *Selected Translations 1948–1968* (1968), for which he won the P.E.N. Translation Prize for 1968, *Transparence of the World*, a translation of his selection of poems by Jean Follain (1969), *Osip Mandelstam, Selected Poems* (with Clarence Brown) (1974) and *Selected Translations 1968–1978*. He has also published three books of prose, *The Miner's Pale Children* (1970), *Houses and Travellers* (1977) and *Unframed Originals* (1982). In 1974 he was awarded The Fellowship of the Academy of American Poets.